AF575381

Jared Siemens and John Willis

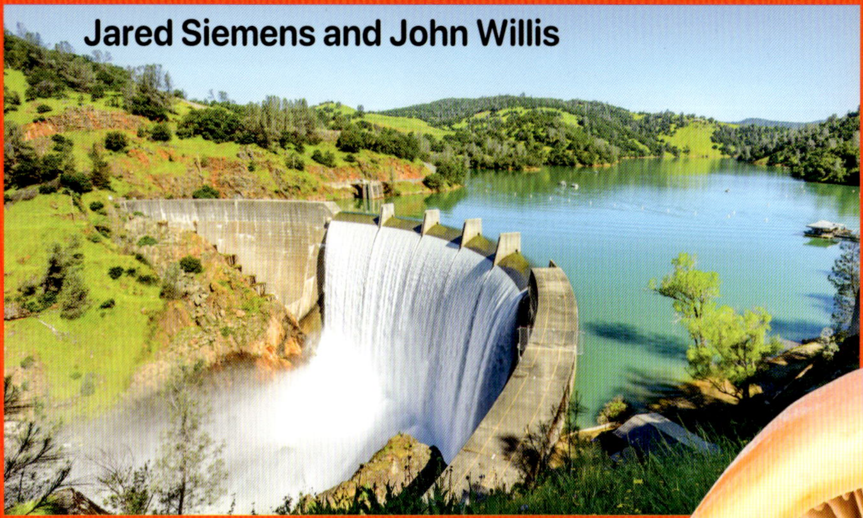

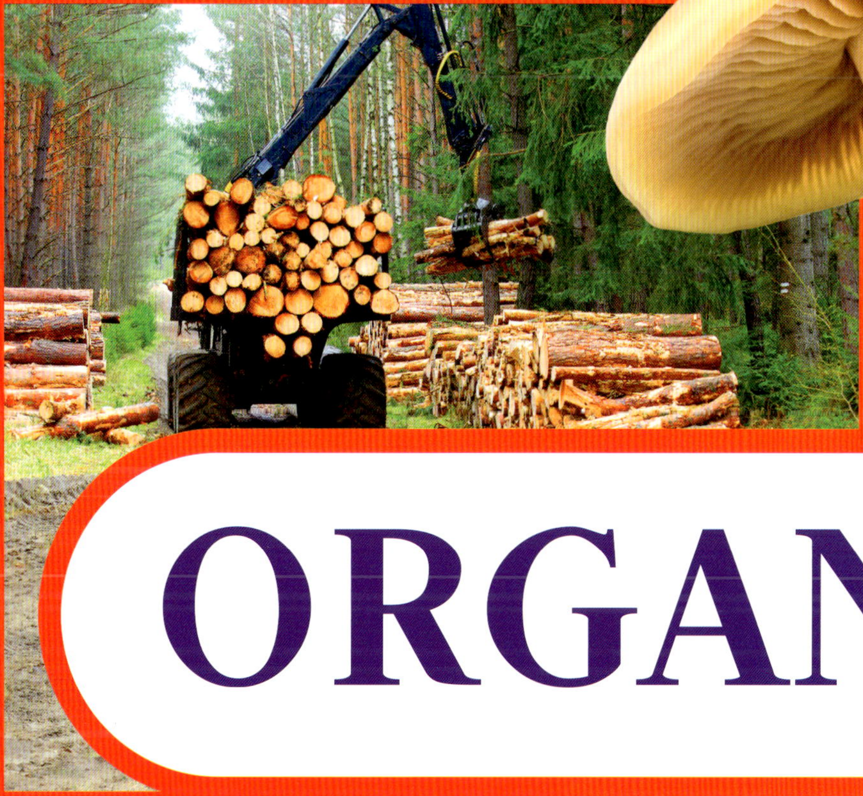

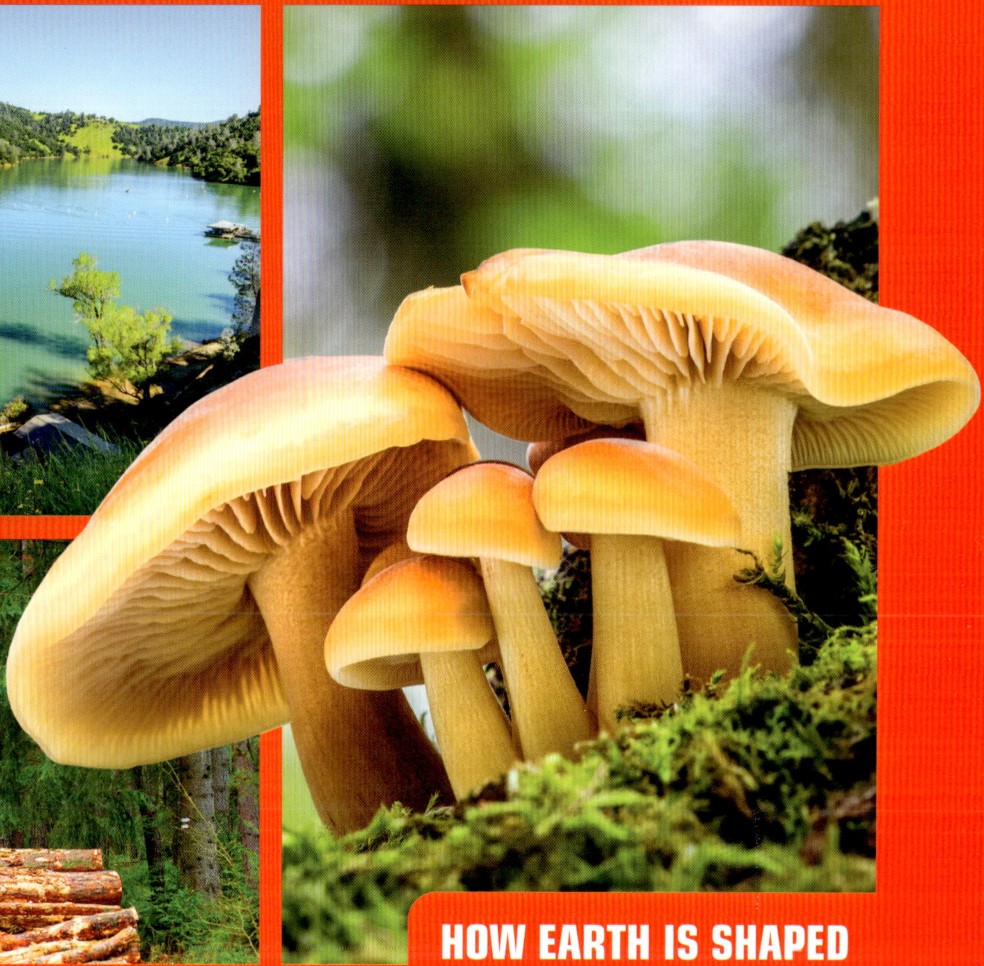

HOW EARTH IS SHAPED

ORGANISMS

LIGHTBOX
openlightbox.com

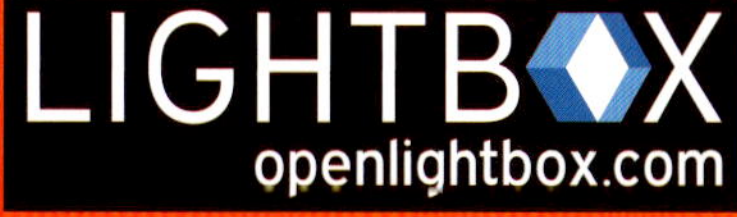

LIGHTBOX

Go to **www.openlightbox.com** and enter this book's unique code.

ACCESS CODE

LBXM2524

Lightbox is an all-inclusive digital solution for the teaching and learning of curriculum topics in an original, groundbreaking way. Lightbox is based on National Curriculum Standards.

OPTIMIZED FOR

- ✓ TABLETS
- ✓ SMART BOARDS
- ✓ COMPUTERS
- ✓ AND MUCH MORE!

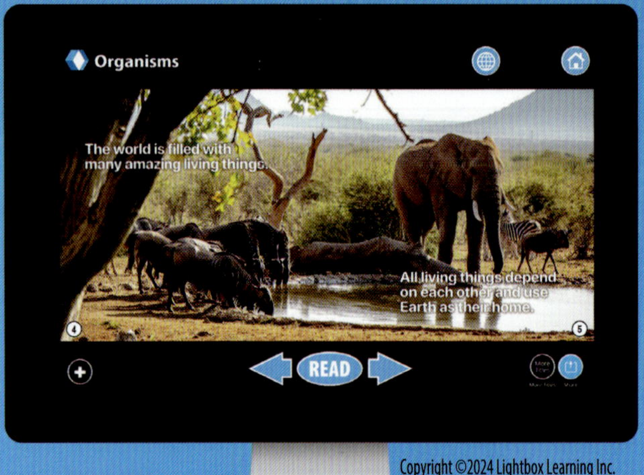

STANDARD FEATURES OF LIGHTBOX

- **AUDIO** High-quality narration using text-to-speech system
- **VIDEOS** Embedded high-definition video clips
- **ACTIVITIES** Printable PDFs that can be emailed and graded
- **WEBLINKS** Curated links to external, child-safe resources
- **SLIDESHOWS** Pictorial overviews of key concepts
- **INTERACTIVE MAPS** Interactive maps and aerial satellite imagery
- **QUIZZES** Ten multiple choice questions that are automatically graded and emailed for teacher assessment
- **KEY WORDS** Matching key concepts to their definitions

SUPPLEMENTARY RESOURCES

- **SHARE** Share titles within your Learning Management System (LMS) or Library Circulation System
- **CURRICULUM** Find national and state curriculum correlations
- **CITATION** Create bibliographical references following APA, CMSO, and MLA styles

VIDEOS

WEBLINKS

SLIDESHOWS

QUIZZES

This title is part of our Lightbox digital subscription

Lightbox Grades K–2 Subscription
ISBN 978-1-5105-5423-8

Access hundreds of Lightbox titles with our digital subscription.
Sign up for a **FREE** subscription trial at **www.openlightbox.com/trial**

The digital components of this book are guaranteed to stay active for at least five years from the date of publication.

ORGANISMS

Contents

The world is filled with many amazing living things.

All living things depend on each other and use Earth as their home.

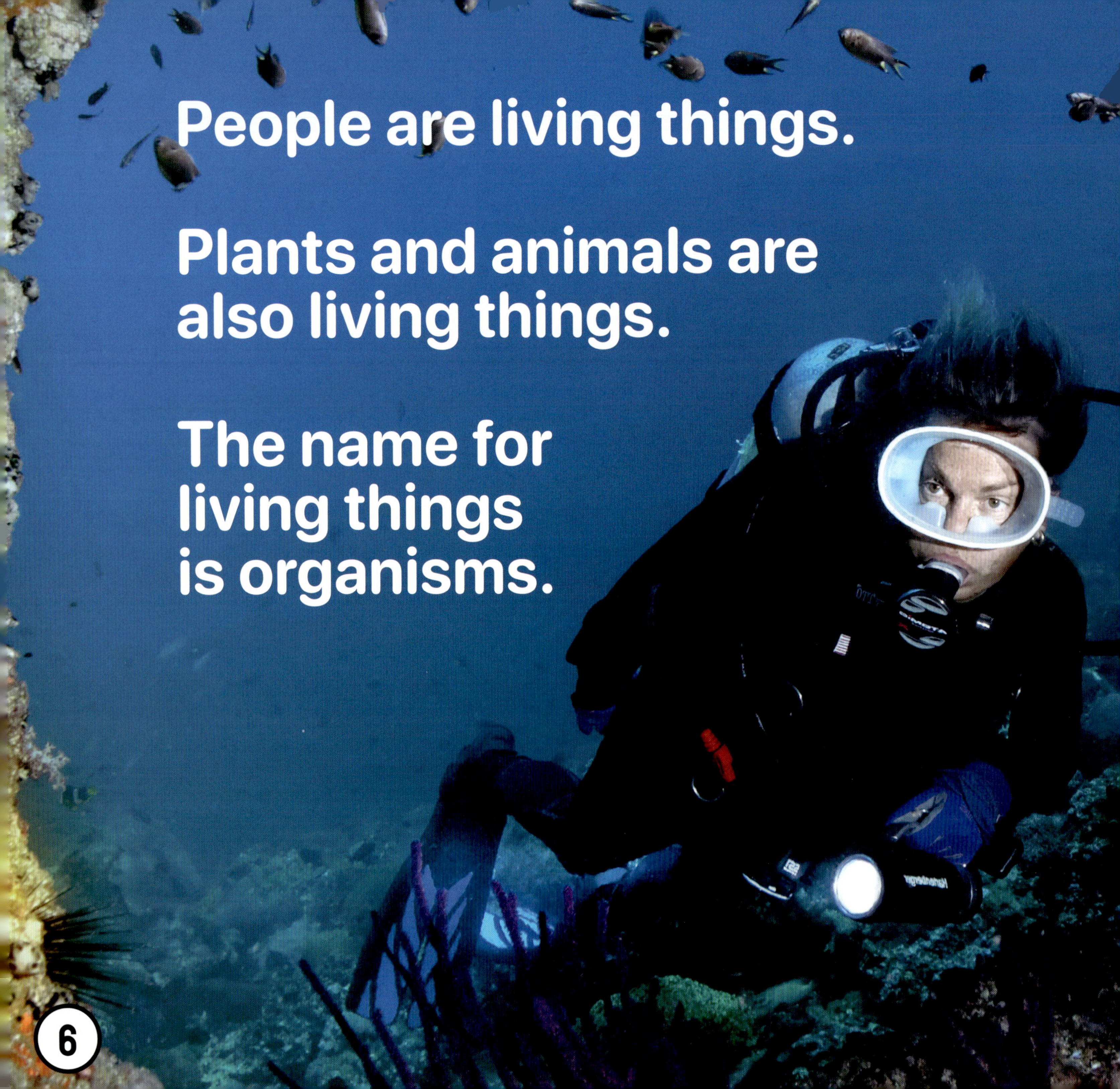

People are living things.

Plants and animals are also living things.

The name for living things is organisms.

In some ways, all organisms are the same.

In other ways, they are very different.

All organisms need water, air, food, and a place to live.

Organisms Belong to a Food Chain

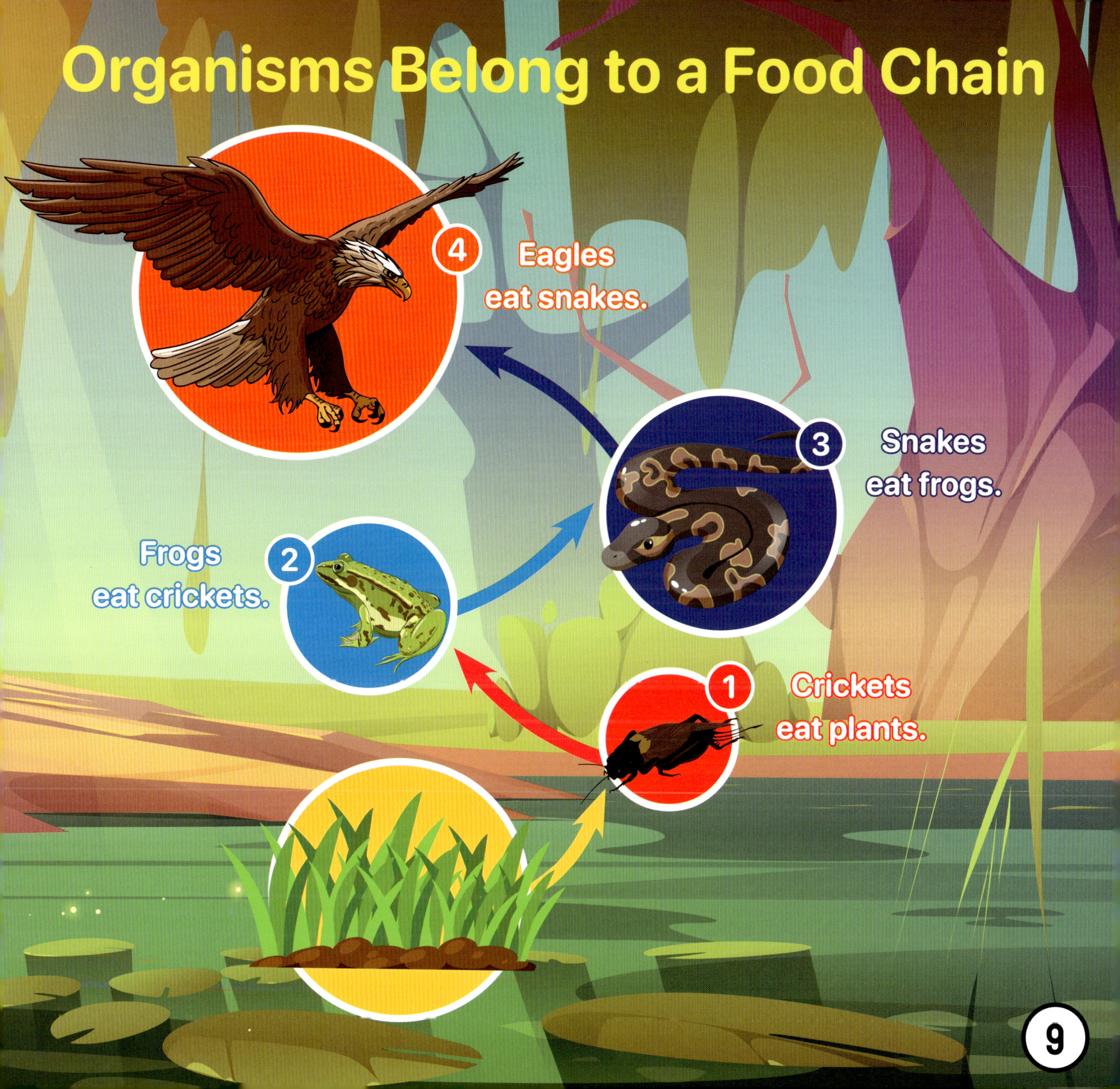

Animals meet their needs in different ways.

Animals that live on land live differently from those that live in water.

Some animals eat plants and animals. Other animals eat only plants.

Plants are
special organisms.

They must have the
light of the Sun in
order to grow.

People and animals
depend on plants
for their food.

Why Do Plants Need Sunlight?

Plants make their own food.

Sunlight

Gas

They take gas from the air and water from the soil.

Their leaves use sunlight to turn the gas and water into food.

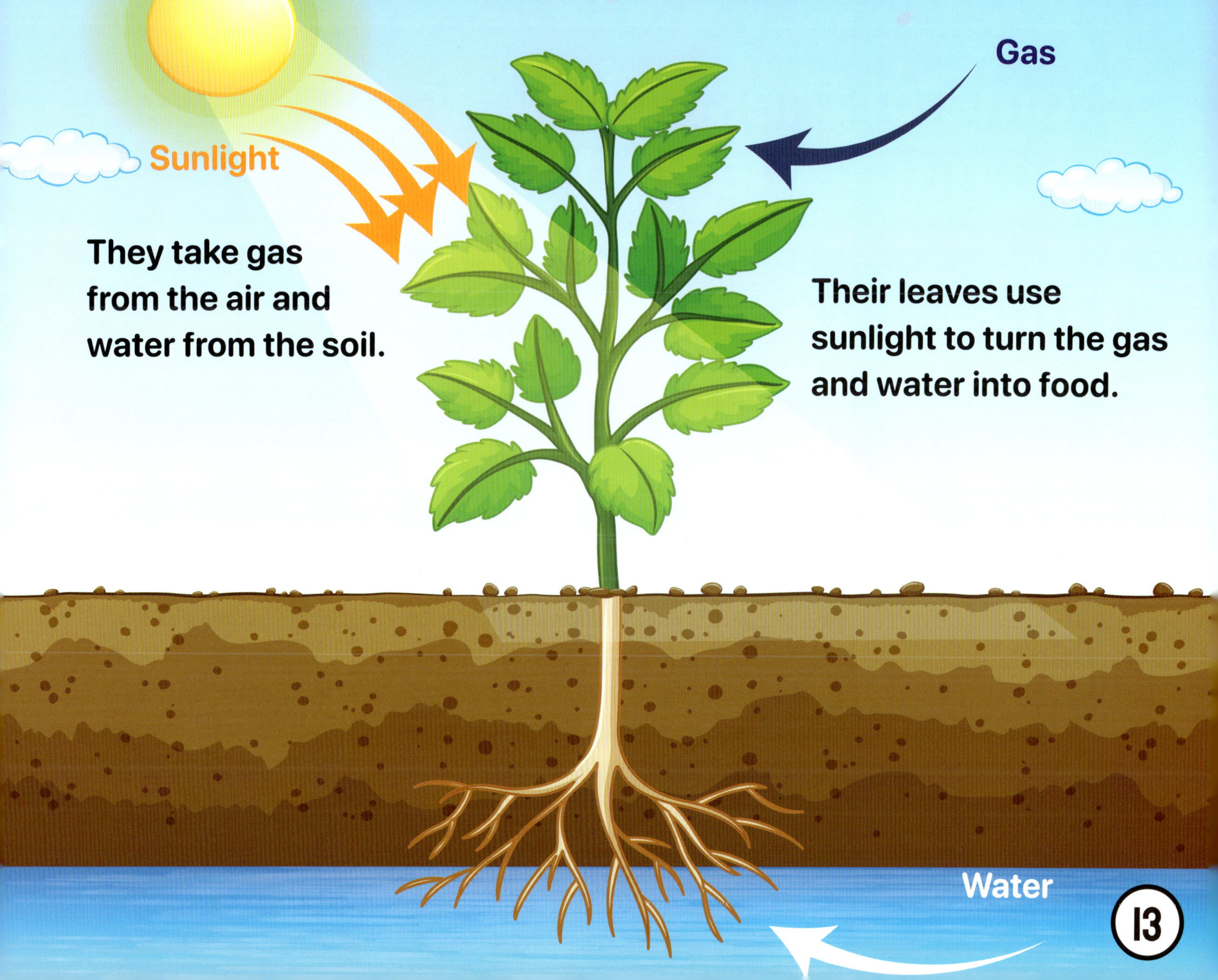

Water

People make choices every day.

Some of these choices can harm the Earth.

Other choices can help keep Earth and living things safe.

People cut down forests and plant crops where trees once grew.

This can leave birds and other forest animals without homes.

Lost Forests

Top four countries for cutting down forests

(2021)

5,979 square miles (15,486 square kilometers)

Brazil

1,927 square miles (4,991 sq. km)

Democratic Republic of the Congo

1,125 square miles (2,914 sq. km)

Bolivia

783 square miles (2,028 sq. km)

Indonesia

Area of forest cut down

People build dams on rivers to make use of the water.

Dams can change the homes of fish that live in rivers.

People celebrate Earth Day every year on April 22.

We can help keep Earth clean by picking up garbage in our neighborhoods.

How can you help Earth and its living things stay healthy?

ORGANISMS FACTS

These pages provide detailed information that expands on the interesting facts found in the book. They are intended to be used by adults as a learning support to help young readers round out their knowledge of each interesting topic featured in the *How Earth Is Shaped* series.

Pages 4–5

Living Things Scientists estimate that there are more than 8 million different species of animals and plants living on Earth. Only about 14 percent of all organisms have been discovered and documented by scientists. Plants and animals interact with each other and with the living and nonliving things in their environments. These interactions create an ecosystem. When people enter into an ecosystem, they need to take care that they do not upset its natural balance.

Pages 6–7

What Are Organisms? All living things are organisms. They react to the world around them. For instance, animals can run from predators and plants can grow towards the light. Organisms are able to reproduce and grow. Humans are organisms. Unlike other organisms, humans can have immense impact on Earth and other living things. Humans have caused the extinction of more than 300 animal species in the last 500 years.

Pages 8–9

What Do Organisms Need? In order to survive, organisms must be able to meet their basic needs. An organism needs an environment with the correct temperature and enough food and water to consume. Most organisms also need to breathe oxygen to live. An organism's cells use oxygen to break down sugars from food. This releases energy that cells need to function. The average human body is about 60 percent water and cannot function properly without regular hydration.

Pages 10–11

Animal Needs Different organisms meet their needs in different ways. Some organisms, such as plants, are producers. Producers are able to make their own food. Other organisms, such as people and other animals, are consumers. They get their food by eating producers or other consumers. Some consumers, such as bears, eat both producers and consumers. Organisms have unique features, such as lungs or gills, which allow them to survive in their environment. These features are called adaptations.

Pages 12–13

Plants Are Special Plants are able to use energy from sunlight in order to create food. This process is called photosynthesis. When plants create food, they also create the oxygen that animals need to breathe. Animals get energy from the plants they eat and pass it on to other animals if they are eaten. In this way, the Sun is responsible for all of the food organisms consume.

Pages 14–15

Organisms Shape the Earth All living things use their environments to meet their needs. This can shape their environments. Humans use and change their environments in order to live more comfortably. More than 80 percent of Earth's land area has been affected in some way by human activity. People build cities and roads that can harm or destroy ecosystems. Other human activities can help the environment. Governments create parks and sanctuaries in order to keep natural environments safe.

Pages 16–17

Cutting Down Trees About 70 percent of land-dwelling plants and animals on Earth live in forests. People use trees to make wood and paper products. Farmers cut down trees in order to make room for crops to grow and livestock to graze. Trees help remove greenhouses gases from the air, slowing global warming. This effect can be diminished when trees are removed from forests. People can help forests regrow by planting new trees after logging.

Pages 18–19

Building Dams People make dams to store drinking water, provide water to crops, and generate electricity. The Hoover Dam creates enough electricity to serve 1.3 million people each year. Dams can make it difficult for fish to migrate upstream to reproduce. People have built devices called fish ladders in order to help fish travel safely past dams. Dams create still reservoirs with different environmental conditions from rivers. This can make it hard for river animals to survive near a dam.

Pages 20–21

Earth Day The first Earth Day was observed in the United States on April 22, 1970. Today, the Earth Day Network works with more than 50,000 partners in 196 countries. More than one billion people take part in Earth Day each year. In 2018, the United States created about 292 million tons (265 million metric tons) of trash. Only 32 percent of this trash was recycled and composted, allowing new products to be created with less waste.

KEY WORDS

Research has shown that as much as 65 percent of all written material published in English is made up of 300 words. These 300 words cannot be taught using pictures or learned by sounding them out. They must be recognized by sight. This book contains 82 common sight words to help young readers improve their reading fluency and comprehension. This book also teaches young readers several important content words, such as proper nouns. These words are paired with pictures to aid in learning and improve understanding.

Page	Sight Words First Appearance
4	is, many, the, things, with, world,
5	all, and, as, each, Earth, home, on, other, their, use
6	also, animals, are, for, name, people, plants
8	a, air, different, food, in, live, need, place, same, some, they, to, very, water, ways
9	eat
11	from, land, only, that, those
12	grow, have, light, must, of,
13	do, into, leaves, make, own, take, turn, why
14	can, day, every, help, keep, these
16	cut, down, once, this, trees, where, without
17	four, miles
18	change, rivers
20	year
21	by, how, its, our, up, we, you

Page	Content Words First Appearance
6	organisms
9	chain, crickets, eagles, frogs, snakes
12	order, Sun
13	gas, soil, sunlight
14	choices
16	birds, crops, forests
17	area, Brazil, Bolivia, countries, Democratic Republic of the Congo, Indonesia
18	dams, fish
20	April
21	garbage, neighborhoods

Published by Lightbox Learning Inc.
276 5th Avenue, Suite 704 #917
New York, NY 10001
Website: www.openlightbox.com

Library of Congress Control Number: 2023942801

ISBN 978-1-5105-6721-4 (hardcover)
ISBN 978-1-5105-6722-1 (multi-user eBook)

Printed in Guangzhou, China
1 2 3 4 5 6 7 8 9 0 27 26 25 24 23

072023
110822

Project Coordinator: Sara Cucini **Designer:** Terry Paulhus

Every reasonable effort has been made to trace ownership and to obtain permission to reprint copyright material. The publisher would be pleased to have any errors or omissions brought to its attention so that they may be corrected in subsequent printings.

The publisher acknowledges Alamy, Getty Images, and Shutterstock as the primary image suppliers for this title.